Odd Jobs

by Sarah Albee
illustrated by Dave Clegg

 A GOLDEN BOOK • NEW YORK

ISBN: 0-307-45453-3

Printed in the United States of America   September 2002

10 9 8 7 6 5 4 3 2 1

In This Book
You Can:

- Write your own stories.

- Illustrate your ideas.

- Brainstorm silly topics.

- Be creative!

BRAINSTORM!

Jobs I'd like to have when I grow up:

1. _____

2. _____

3. _____

4. _____

5. _____

Pick one.

Why would you like to have that job?

_____

_____

_____

_____

_____

BRAINSTORM!

Jobs I would NOT like to have when I grow up:

1. _____

2. _____

3. _____

4. _____

5. _____

Pick one.
Why would you NOT like to have
that job?

_____

_____

_____

_____

_____

Write a letter explaining why you're the best person for *this* job.

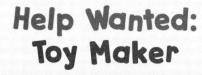

Help Wanted:
Toy Maker

Must be short, handy with tools, and able to work under pressure. Also, must like cold weather. If interested, please write to Mr. S. Claus, The North Pole.

Date: _____

Dear Mr. Claus:

_____

_____

_____

_____

_____

_____

_____

Sincerely yours,

_____

· ZOOKEEPER ·

Explain to your new assistant
how to feed the sharks.

First, _____

_____

_____

Then, _____

_____

_____

Be careful not to _____

_____

_____

Finally, _____

_____

_____

· CHEF ·

You're the chef at a new restaurant that's just for kids. What's on the menu?

* Menu *

_____

_____

_____

_____

_____

_____

Make a list of things that are NOT on the menu.

_____

_____

_____

_____

_____

_____

_____

_____

_____

_____

· INVENTOR ·

Imagine you've invented something
that makes doing chores more fun.
What is it called?
How does it work?

_____

_____

_____

_____

_____

_____

_____

_____

_____

Draw your invention.

·ATHLETE·

Make a list of your favorite sports.

_____   _____

_____   _____

_____   _____

If you were a famous athlete,
which of those sports would you
want to play?

_____

_____

_____

_____

· WRITER ·

Describe a recent game for the newspaper's sports page.

SPORTS

_____
_____
_____
_____
_____
_____
_____
_____
_____
_____
_____

· SECRETARY ·

You're the Tooth Fairy's secretary.
She didn't pick up a kid's tooth last night.
List some possible reasons why
she didn't show up.

_____

_____

_____

_____

_____

_____

Write a letter of apology.

Date: _____

Dear _____:

_____

_____

_____

_____

_____

_____

Sincerely yours,

_____

Secretary to the Tooth Fairy

· NEWSCASTER ·

You're on live at 5:00.
Report today's news.

In local news, _____

_____

_____

_____

_____

In national news, _____

_____

_____

_____

_____

In world news, _____

_____

_____

_____

_____

In sports, _____

_____

_____

_____

The weather tomorrow will be

_____

_____

_____

_____

BRAINSTORM!

My favorite things to do:

1. _____

2. _____

3. _____

4. _____

5. _____

Choose one thing from your list. What kind of job would allow you to do your favorite thing?

_____

_____

_____

_____

_____

_____

· ASTRONAUT ·

You just got back
from outer space.
Write about your trip in
your travel journal.

First, _____

_____

_____

It was _____

_____

_____

_____

Next, _____

_____

_____

It was _____

_____

_____

Then, _____

_____

_____

I felt _____

_____

_____

Finally, _____

_____

_____

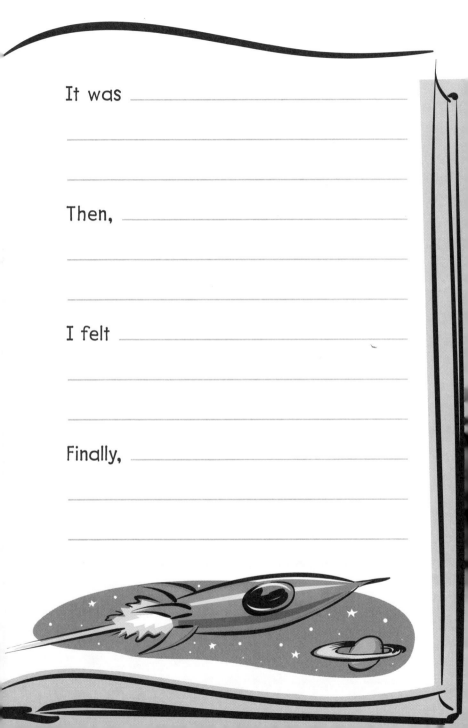

· CREATIVE DIRECTOR ·

You need to make an ad for
a new frozen dinner product—
*Liver & Onions with Yucky
Green Stuff on the Side.*
List five reasons why your
product is terrific.

1. _____

2. _____

3. _____

4. _____

5. _____

Draw the ad.

Write a letter explaining why you're the best person for *this* job.

Help Wanted: Referee

Must be quick footed, good at problem solving, and able to work with all types of people.
If interested, please write to Yule B. Sorry.

Date: _____

Dear Mr. Sorry:

_____

_____

_____

_____

_____

_____

_____

Sincerely yours,

_____

· SCIENTIST ·

You've just discovered a rare
new species of lizard.
Describe it.

It looks like _____

_____

It's as big as a _____

_____

It lives in _____

_____

It eats _____

_____

Make up your own question.

My question is: _____

_____

_____

_____

Answer: _____

_____

_____

_____

· REPORTER ·

You're interviewing the Three Bears.
What questions will you ask them?

_____

_____

_____

_____

_____

_____

_____

_____

It gets angry when _____

_____

When it's angry, it _____

_____

It's happy when _____

_____

Draw your new discovery.

· INTERVIEWER ·

Ask someone you know to answer
these questions:

What do you do? _____

_____

What is the best thing about your job?

_____

_____

What is the worst thing about your job?

_____

_____

When you were a kid, what did you

want to be? _____

_____

_____

Write your article.

BREAK-IN AT LOCAL COTTAGE!

Golden-haired girl in custody!

925912618

_____

_____

_____

_____

_____

_____

_____

_____

_____

BRAINSTORM!

My favorite circus acts:

1._____

2._____

3._____

4._____

5._____

Pick one.
Imagine performing that circus act.
Write about it.

_____

_____

_____

_____

_____

_____

· SONGWRITER ·

You write jingles for commercials.
Write down words that make you
think of laundry soap.

Write a song
about laundry soap.
When you're done, try singing it.

_____

_____

_____

_____

_____

_____

_____

_____

_____

_____

_____

· PRINCIPAL ·

You're the principal of your school!
Make up some new rules.

_____

_____

_____

_____

_____

_____

_____

Make a list of rules that kids no longer need to obey.

_____

_____

_____

_____

_____

_____

_____

· PILOT ·

Describe a typical day of flying.

First, _____

_____

_____

Then, _____

_____

_____

Finally, _____

_____

_____

Draw what you see from the air.

Write about your morning chores.

When I woke up, I _____

Then, I _____

_____

_____

_____

_____

_____

_____

_____

_____

_____

Finally, it was time for breakfast.

· SUBSTITUTE TEACHER ·

Your teacher has come down
with chicken pox!
You have to teach the class today.
Write down some things
you're good at.

_____

_____

_____

_____

_____

Choose one thing from your list.
Teach the class how to do it.

First, _____

_____

Then, _____

_____

Next, _____

_____

Finally, _____

_____

·THE PRESIDENT·

Imagine you're the president.
Write three things you would do
to improve the country.

1. _____

2. _____

3. _____